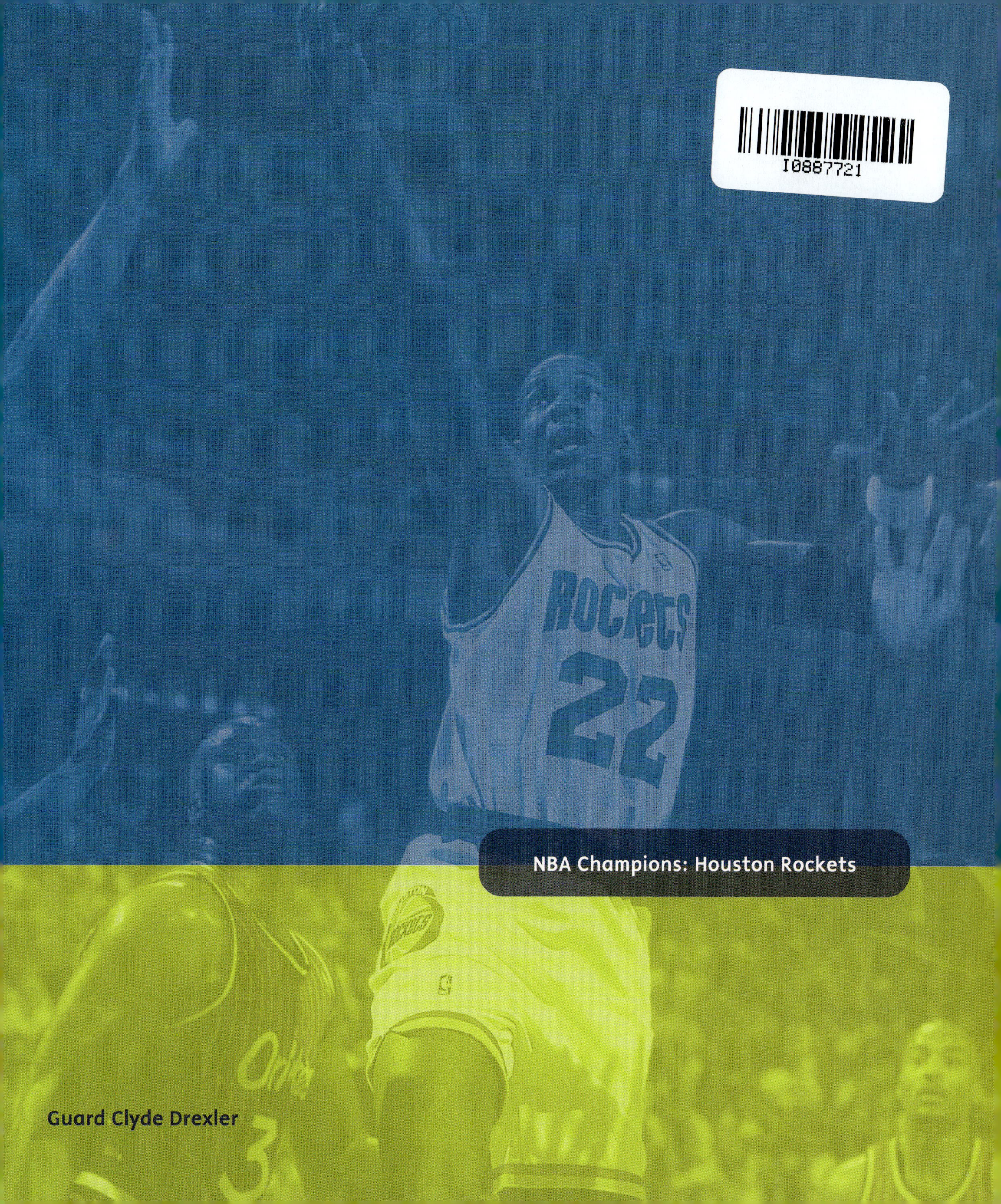

NBA Champions: Houston Rockets

Guard Clyde Drexler

Guard Robert Reid

NBA CHAMPIONS

HOUSTON ROCKETS

BY JAMES BARRY

CREATIVE EDUCATION / CREATIVE PAPERBACKS

Center Moses Malone

Published by Creative Education and Creative Paperbacks
P.O. Box 227, Mankato, Minnesota 56002
Creative Education and Creative Paperbacks are imprints of
The Creative Company
www.thecreativecompany.us

Art Direction by Tom Morgan
Book production by Graham Morgan
Edited by Grace Cain

Images by Getty Images/Al Bello, 20, Andrew D. Bernstein, 7, 12, 16, Bill Baptist, 5, Dick Raphael, 2, 15, 19, Jamie Sabau, 24, John W. McDonough, 1, Nathaniel S. Butler, 3, 6, Thearon W. Henderson, cover, Tim Warner, 10, Unknown, 9, Vernon Biever, cover, 4
Every effort has been made to contact copyright holders for material reproduced in this book. Any omissions will be rectified in subsequent printings if notice is given to the publisher.

Library of Congress Cataloging-in-Publication Data

Names: Barry, James (author of children's books), author.
Title: Houston Rockets / by James Barry.
Description: Mankato, Minnesota : Creative Education and Creative Paperbacks, [2025] | Series: Creative Sports: NBA champions | ATOS: 3.7. | Audience: Ages 7-10 years | Audience: Grades 2-3 | Summary: "Elementary-level text and dynamic sports photos highlight the NBA championship wins of the Houston Rockets, plus sensational players associated with the professional basketball team such as Jalen Green"— Provided by publisher.
Identifiers: LCCN 2024014669 (print) | LCCN 2024014670 (ebook) | ISBN 9798889892571 (library binding) | ISBN 9781682776230 (paperback) | ISBN 9798889893684 (ebook)
Subjects: LCSH: Houston Rockets (Basketball team)—History—Juvenile literature. | Basketball—Texas—Houston—History—Juvenile literature.
Classification: LCC GV885.52.H68 B37 2025 (print) | LCC GV885.52.H68 (ebook) | DDC 796.323/64097641411—dc23/eng/20240418
LC record available at https://lccn.loc.gov/2024014669
LC ebook record available at https://lccn.loc.gov/2024014670

Printed in China

Forward Luis Scola

Guard Mario Elie

CONTENTS

Home of the Rockets 8

Naming the Rockets 13

Rockets History 14

Other Rockets Stars 18

About the Rockets 22

Glossary 23

Index 24

NBA CHAMPIONS

Home of the Rockets

Houston, Texas, is the largest city in the southern United States. It is big in the oil and gas industry. The city is known as "The Energy Capital of the World." Houston has an **arena** called the Toyota Center. It is the home of a basketball team called the Rockets.

Guard Jalen Green

The Houston Rockets are a team in the National Basketball Association (NBA). They play in the Southwest Division. That's part of the Western Conference. Their **rivals** are the Dallas Mavericks and the San Antonio Spurs. All NBA teams want to win the NBA Finals and become champions.

Forward Robert Horry

Naming the Rockets

The team began in San Diego, California. This city is home to space studies and education. When the team moved to Houston, the owners kept the name. That seemed like a good idea. Houston is where astronauts train to take rockets into space.

Rockets History

The Rockets started playing in 1967. They won very few games at first. The team's best player was legendary big man Elvin Hayes. He led the NBA in scoring in his first year with the Rockets.

In 1971, the Rockets moved to Houston. Center Moses Malone joined the team in 1976. He helped them get to the **playoffs** four years in a row. Malone won two **Most Valuable Player (MVP)** awards with Houston. In 1981, the Rockets reached the NBA Finals. They lost to the Boston Celtics.

Forward Elvin Hayes

Center Hakeem Olajuwon

In 1984, the Rockets made an important choice. They chose center Hakeem Olajuwon with the first overall pick in the NBA Draft. He was a great scorer and one of the best shot blockers ever. He led the Rockets to NBA championships in 1994 and 1995.

The Rockets have not won any more **titles**. They have had winning seasons most years. In the 2000s, Houston fans enjoyed watching 7-foot-6 center Yao Ming and skillful guard Tracy McGrady. High-scoring guard James Harden joined the Rockets in 2012. He won the MVP award in 2018.

Other Rockets Stars

Two of the Rockets' first stars were forward Rudy Tomjanovich and guard Calvin Murphy. Tomjanovich later coached the Rockets to their back-to-back championships. At 5 foot 9, Murphy ran fast and sank shot after shot.

Guard Calvin Murphy

Guard Fred VanVleet

Forward Ralph Sampson was named NBA Rookie of the Year in 1984. He was an All-Star in his first four seasons with the Rockets.

In 2023, the Rockets added steady guard Fred VanVleet. He joined center Alperen Şengün and guard Jalen Green. Fans hope they can form another title team soon!

About the Rockets

First season: 1967–68

Conference/division: Western Conference, Southwest Division

Team colors: red, silver, black, and white

Home arena: Toyota Center

NBA CHAMPIONSHIPS:

1994, 4 games to 3 over New York Knicks

1995, 4 games to 0 over Orlando Magic

TEAM WEBSITE:

https://www.nba.com/rockets

Glossary

arena—a large building with seats for spectators, where sports games and entertainment events are held

Most Valuable Player (MVP)—an honor given to the season's best player

playoffs—games that the best teams play after a regular season to see who the champion will be

rival—a team that plays extra hard against another team

title—another word for championship

Center Alperen Şengün

Index

Green, Jalen, 10, 21
Harden, James, 17
Hayes, Elvin, 14, 15
Horry, Robert, 12
Malone, Moses, 14
McGrady, Tracy, 17
Ming, Yao, 17
Murphy, Calvin, 18, 19
Olajuwon, Hakeem, 16, 17
Sampson, Ralph, 21
Şengün, Alperen, 21, 24
team name, 8, 13
Tomjanovich, Rudy, 18
Toyota Center, 8, 22
VanVleet, Fred, 20, 21